Little Acts of Decluttering

By Rachel Noakes

with thanks to friends and family for
always being my biggest cheerleaders.

Contents

Introduction

It may surprise you to know that I used to be a hoarder. If I could show you my teenage bedroom, set in the late 90s/early 00s, you would be horrified. Shocked to the core. I kept everything: books, photos, ornaments, old school books, letters, birthday cards, Christmas cards and I was in the box room. The tiny, above the stair bedroom. It surprises me, still, how much stuff I could fit in there.

Since moving out at 18 and living in several flats and houses since, I continued to lug my junk around, like we all do. Fast forward to my 30s, and life has a whole different meaning. A person close to me said that I was 'too messy'. At the time, I was a little chaotic, in my first term as a NQT, but I was generally NOT that messy...I would argue that it was organised chaos. I knew exactly where everything was and I was happy with that. For a while. Teaching takes its toll, as you can imagine.

Coming home from work, completing chores and keeping the house tidy has always felt overwhelming for me, especially as a single mum. My home felt chaotic and my health was deteriorating due to developing chronic fatigue syndrome. Tidy home, tidy mind immediately came to me and I knew I had to make a change. A journey was about to begin and little did I know how impactful it would become.

Alongside this came a necessity to clear my debt; from student overdrafts, credit cards and hire purchase loans. I began selling stuff I didn't need to help pay off the debt. I started with more valuable items, jewellery, furniture and electronic devices. Every penny helped to chip away at the debt. But something bigger happened. I started to feel a change. My environment became a little calmer, a little easier to manage and took far less time to clean. Timed with the beginning of minimalist shows on streaming sites, such as The Minimalist, The Home Edit and Tidying up with Marie Kondo, my whole mindset changed. It was freeing.

Decluttering is something I have done regularly, mostly due to regular house moves, but I am fully aware of how overwhelming a task it can be. At first I was able to declutter whole rooms in a day and feel like I had made big strides. But after a while, chronic fatigue became a part of my life and so I had to start pacing myself. I realised, after decluttering my whole house, that I still had too much stuff! Reality sunk in. I had been far too generous the first time round and was keeping things that I still didn't need. It was time for round 2. This time I did things a little slower and thought carefully about each item and category that I was working in. I starting asking myself questions and it became much easier to part with my items.

It's now 2 years down the line and my home is full of beautiful things that I love. I carefully consider anything that I bring into my home and I have shared my journey on my social media pages. In doing so, I realised that, like me, not everyone could take on a whole room at a time when letting go of items from their home. Little acts of decluttering was born during my later decluttering days as I was trying to chip away slowly due to my deteriorating health. A way of chunking up different areas to declutter in a more manageable way. Each little act focuses on one area or type of item to allow you to make small steps towards a bigger change.

So here we are, at the beginning of your journey. A moment in which you have taken the first step towards a less cluttered home. I am not here to preach or convert you towards minimalism (although do read around the topic). I am here to help you create the home you want and deserve.

Motivation to Declutter

Know Your Why

Before we get started, we need to get motivated. The first type of motivation is knowing your 'why'. Why do you want to remove items from your home and what are you hoping to achieve? Your why is going to be the reminder you never knew you needed. It's not just about having less, it is about curating a home that makes you feel good. So you need to know what makes you feel good!

Visualisation

The second type of motivation is visualising your goal, the end result. Having a visual goal to aim for will inspire you to keep going. What will the end result look like? Are you aiming for Instagram worthy or is it a more practical approach that means your home is manageable? Knowing what the end goal looks like will help you to know when you've reached it. It's a feeling that you will just sense is there. I suppose it's a 'trust the process' moment. You will know when you feel like you have achieved your goal.

Before and After Photos

If you want to keep tabs on your progress and see the results, before and after photos will be perfect for you. Seeing your start point and being able to reflect after clearing out and decluttering the space is going to give you that dopamine hit to keep going. It will spur you to keep going and continue working in other areas. This is also something you could share with friends and family.

Declutter Buddy

This one is great for those that need the emotional support when decluttering. Having a friend or family member who will cheer you on, motivate you and keep you accountable is a fantastic way to enjoy the decluttering process. It's not going to be an easy journey and having someone to share that with will make it a little easier. Choose someone that is either likeminded and wants to declutter their home too, or someone that knows you really well who will be the emotional support for those difficult items that are harder to let go of. They will keep you in check and help you to see things from a different perspective.

Little By Little

No one is asking you to sort your house out in a day. There may be different reasons why this may be needed, but as far as I am concerned, little by little is my approach. Keep it simple and work in a small area at a time. How small is entirely up to you. You may wish to do the whole wardrobe at once, or you may wish to work one section or drawer at a time. You have the ownership on this one.

Challenges

I will go into this in more detail in another chapter, but challenges are a great way to get motivated to declutter. There are a range of different ones that might peak your interest, the 30 day minimalism game, the 12-12-12 challenge, 10 minutes-10 spaces-100 items. You could try a timer or give yourself a number of items to find. The aim is purely to make it fun and take away the pressure of having to do a large amount of decluttering in one go. 15 items or 15 minutes is a great way to keep chipping away at cluttered areas of your home.

Set Achievable Goals

Goal setting is another favourite pastime of mine. It's a motivator in itself, knowing you have a goal to achieve. If you want to be successful, make them smart. Make sure the goals are small and achievable, with actions written down that will help you to achieve it. Consider what might be your barriers to being able to complete the goal and factor in ideas to overcome this.

Reality Check

Money Down The Drain

It may surprise you to hear this, but your 'stuff' is not worth as much as you think. That £400 sofa will only be worth £40 on local selling sites. Items are only worth what someone is willing to pay. And the price can vary.

If it's not a collectable then it is worth nothing. Yet we continue to represent that item in our minds at the price we originally paid. It's why it becomes so hard to let go. We don't want to let go of a perceived value when the reality states that it's worth £2 at best. Try not to think of it as money down the drain. That value that you associate can be passed on in a different way. The value of purposefulness.

Emotional Toll

At no point am I going to say that this is easy. There are going to be items that will test you and potentially feel like they are holding you back. These sentimental items will be different for each and every one of you. Some may find clothes too tough with the expectations of weight gain or loss; whilst others may have old toys from childhood. I have dedicated a chapter towards sentimental items. Just know that you can keep whatever is important to you. You have the power to keep anything that makes you happy!

The Basics

Before we get started, there are some key points I need to mention so that you are set up for success.

Donate, Sell, Keep and Trash

For the ease of working in a small area at a time. Having a dedicated box or bag for each of these four categories is going to make tidying up a doddle. If you have a box dedicated to items to sell, it will mean that it is contained at the point of decluttering and is ready to put onto selling sites at your earliest convenience. Trash should be going straight into a bin bag. Don't create extra jobs by creating piles that then need to be moved into a container or bag. Put rubbish straight into a bag so that when you have finished the area, you can take it straight out into the wheelie bin! Job done! Items for donating should be put into a container that can easily be taken to a charity shop. Any items being kept (depending on what they are) can either be put in a pile or put in a box and then put away at the end of the sorting process. This is an opportunity to organise your possessions in a way that is suitable for how you use each item. Make sure that everything has a home and that home needs to be thought about and represent how and where you use the item. This helps things become easier to find and more importantly, quick to put away.

Kitchen

Wine glasses

It can be easy to amass a collection of wine glasses. These are a popular wedding or house warming gift. I collected many from birthday and Christmas presents, including ones with age birthdays or 'best friend' stamped on the side. Lovely at the time, but is it realistic to keep a happy 18th wine glass at 36? I kid you not, I have only just donated this (still in its packaging). It has survived six house moves in that time. Consider thinking about having a number of glasses that you will likely use that suit your home and donate or sell the remainder.

Baking Trays

Hands up, who is still collecting and using baking trays that are peeling and not fit for purpose? That used to be me too! It is absolutely ok to buy a new baking tray, as and when, but remember to recycle the old. Think about the meals you make and only keep trays that will be used or that serve a purpose, such as Yorkshire pudding or muffin trays.

Kitchen Appliances

Do you like to keep up with the latest trends, buying toastie makers, waffle makers, slow cookers and air fryers? Now ask yourself 'are you still using them?' If you have unused appliances, these are taking up valuable space in your cupboards or on your counter tops. These are good items to sell to earn some extra money or donate to friends and family that might want to try them out.

Saucepans

How often do you reach for the same saucepan, whilst the others sit in the cupboard never used for various reasons, such as having a dodgy handle, or the non-stick has gone? Yet we still keep it in the cupboard! It's time to keep only the essentials. Saucepans take up a lot of space and you only need the amount you are likely to use at one time.

Water Bottles

Do you have a collection of water bottles in a drawer, including ones that leak? It's time to keep only the number that you need for the number of people in the family. A water bottle is fantastic for carrying around, so make sure the ones you keep fit into the side pockets of your bags, have a comfortable handle and are easy to clean.

Travel Mugs

I used to have a number of travel mugs. Some were great, whilst others would have dodgy lids or were difficult to drink from. It's time to keep your favourite and declutter the rest. I only need one travel drinking mug for school for hot drinks, and that's it. Keep what is essential to you.

Cutlery

It can be easy to become ladened with cutlery. You may buy extra cutlery sets to save having to keep on top of the washing up, but this can complicate things and make the cutlery drawer feel overwhelming. Be realistic and reduce down what you have. It is easy enough to clean cutlery ready for use again.

Kitchen Sink

This is often stacked with cleaning sprays, washing supplies and overflowing with tea towels. It can be a catch all area of products. A spray for each room in the house. It is worth considering a multipurpose spray that can be used anywhere. Reduce down the tea towel collection to be the number you would use over a couple of days, knowing these can be regularly washed each week.

Food Containers

This could be a drawer, two drawers or a whole cupboard full of containers and a selection of lids that might fit. You now need to narrow down your food container collection. Only keep ones with lids that fit. Any spare parts should be recycled. You then need to consider which size containers you use the most and if there are some that you are unlikely to use.

Plates and Bowls

Feeding the 5000 or do you just have small dinner parties? Be realistic about how many plates and bowls you really use or need on a daily basis. If you regularly have dinner parties, think about how many you would normally cater for. Do you have a set of plates for special occasions? Every day should be a special occasion and surely you deserve to use them! Make sure you take out any that are chipped or no longer suit your style.

Party Supplies

It can be easy to get caught up in an array of special events that require separate party supplies. hen parties, birthdays and Christmas. Be more intentional with supplies and keep only generic items that could be used for any occasion.

Magnets/Front of Fridge

Holidays and trips out for me always used to be about collecting fridge magnets and displaying them on the front of the fridge. Add life into the mix and you end up storing invitations, notes, photos and children's artwork on the fridge door. This can be overwhelming to look at for some and could be simplified to improve the look of your kitchen. I have previously used picture frames on the wall to show off children's artwork with a 1 in 1 out policy attached.

Use Up Food

Before you start the weekly shop, think about what you already have in your cupboards that might need using up and, more importantly, plan meals from this. This will save you money and prevent any food waste. Another tip for success is to put newly purchased items at the back of the cupboards and bring the older items to the front so that you can see and use them.

Expired Food

An easy way to clear some space in a cluttered kitchen is to remove any expired food. Whilst you can start avoiding this by getting in the habit of regularly using up food and meal planning from stock, it is important to have a regular check of the cupboards. You could go through one shelf at a time whilst cooking dinner to keep on top of things. This will definitely free up some valuable cupboard space.

Washi Tape Strategy

If you're not sure which utensils to declutter from your home you could use the Washi tape strategy. Put a piece of Washi tape on the handle of every cooking utensils. As you use them and wash them, remove the Washi tape. After a period of time (as chosen by you), it will be clear as to which items are being used regularly and those that are not.

Unused Cookbooks

Cookbooks, I feel, is one of those use or lose situations. If you never reach for a particular cookbook is it worth keeping? Kitchen space is always valuable and do you want it to be taken up with items that you don't use or need? In a time when it is so easy to search up recipes, do we need to keep physical copies? If the books are no longer of interest, see if you can donate or sell them on. They are likely to keep some value.

Mugs, Cups and Beakers

If you have children, you may have an endless supply of plastic cups, bottles and glassware. This is an area that needs far fewer items than you think. With the exception of baby bottles (where you do need a decent number ready for use), it can be pretty easy to maintain a smaller number of cups as they are so easy to wash at the sink and be ready to use.

Takeaway Menus

I used to have a collection of takeaway menus by the phone in my 20s. But thankfully, those bundles of joy have moved into an app or website menu, which has everything you could possibly need to make an order from. It's time to recycle the paper copies.

Shopping Bags

Do you have a collection of carrier bags or bags for life being stored in the kitchen cupboards or under the sink? It's time to sift through and keep only what you are likely to use. Any thin plastic bags could be used as liners to pedal bins. Decide whether you want to keep the bags in the kitchen or stored in the boot of the car (if you have one) ready for use.

Kitchen Side Clear

Regularly clearing away the kitchen side can dramatically improve the look of the kitchen. Any appliances that are not used regularly could be put in cupboards so that you have plenty of clear surface areas that are then easy to keep clean.

Tea Towels

An overflowing drawer or a pile under the sink. The chances are, you have more than you need. I have gone with 7 – one for each day of the week and I chuck them straight in the washing machine when they are finished with each day so that they get washed and ready to use again in time. Keep ones that are absorbent and dispose of any that are past their best.

KITCHEN
CHECKLIST

- ☐ wine glasses
- ☐ baking trays
- ☐ kitchen appliances
- ☐ sauce pans
- ☐ water bottles
- ☐ travel mugs
- ☐ cutlery
- ☐ food containers
- ☐ plates and bowls
- ☐ party supplies
- ☐ magnets / front of fridge
- ☐ use up food
- ☐ expired food
- ☐ washi tape strategy
- ☐ unused cook books
- ☐ mugs, cups and beakers
- ☐ take away menus
- ☐ kitchen sink
- ☐ shopping bags
- ☐ kitchen side clear
- ☐ tea towels

Laundry

Laundry

One way to keep on top of the clothing edit is to regularly check items as you are washing and drying them and if you notice they are damaged and unrepairable then these are easy ones to remove. Also, look out for any that shrink in the wash!

Washing Away

As soon as the laundry is dry get in the habit of putting it away immediately. Letting the washing pile up can make it a bigger and more daunting task than it needs to be. Keep it manageable by keeping on top of things.

Cleaning Supplies

Do you have a selection of cleaning products for different rooms in the house? Why not use up the products you have and slimline your future purchases to one multipurpose product?

Washing Supplies

Your clothes washing routine may involve a number of different products; hangers, fabric conditioners, air dryers, steamers. Go through and see whether there are any items that you don't use on a regular basis. Can you survive with the others? Only keep products you like using and donate the rest.

LAUNDRY CHECKLIST

- [ ] laundry
- [ ] washing away
- [ ] cleaning supplies
- [ ] washing supplies

Bathroom

Travel Sized Products

I am totally guilty of doing this in the past. I would collect up all of the little sample sized products during hotel stays with the intention of using them for my next holiday. And did I? Absolutely not, because like most women I like to take a travel sized version of the shampoo that is actually good for my hair. We don't even use them up at home! So it's time to stop taking the sample products and get in the habit of using up any that we do have ASAP.

Expired Bath/Body Products

Bath and body products have an expiry date. This is important because, if like me, you have sensitive skin, it is possible to react if the product is old. Particularly if the item has been opened. Usually these products have a recommended shelf life once opened. So do check the bottles and work out whether it has been open for too long.

Expired Medicine

There are many reasons why it might not be good to keep old medicines. I don't think you need me to list them all; keeping them away from children is one of them. Any opened, unused or expired medicine can be taken to your pharmacy for safe disposal. Any cardboard boxes and paper inserts can be recycled.

Old/Used Sunscreen

For any sensitive skin people out there, this one is particularly important. Each summer, it is important to use a new bottle of sunscreen. Sunscreen is often found left out in the sun and exposed to hot temperatures so it can cause a reaction if used a year later, particularly if you have sensitive skin. The easiest way to know is to dispose of any sunscreen that has been opened at the end of summer. Any unopened bottles should be fine, but always check for expiry dates.

Toiletries/Perfumes

The ten sets of toiletries received at Christmas each year can really start to add up, particularly if you don't use them. You either need to get into the habit of using them straight away, or donate or sell them. Be realistic about what you will actually use from the gift sets and dispose of anything that you know you won't use.

Use Up Products

Some people like to keep a stock of products in the cupboards. But realistically we don't need that many. One of each, as a backup for bathroom related items, should be enough. It will save you some pennies if you start using up what you already have first.

Under the Sink

It can be easy to shove things in the cupboard under the sink and forget about them. I used to have a storage unit full of random stuff, but now I am much more selective about what is kept here: bathroom related items only. Make sure to keep cleaning sprays out of the reach of children or ensure that the cupboard is lockable.

Sink Area

Leaving things around the sink is so easily done and a difficult habit to break. Clear away anything unnecessary and put this in the cupboard under the sink (now that you have made room) so that the visual clutter in the space has been removed.

Towels

I think everyone has a different number of acceptable towels. I have enough for one each and each bathroom and a few spares. They are not all coordinated or matching, but that's fine with me. It's more about how they feel and whether they absorb. But if you are overrun with towels, then decide what is an appropriate number of towels per person for a week and for hand towels in the bathrooms, and dispose of the rest. Animals shelters will take towels and sheets for bedding.

BATHROOM CHECKLIST

- [ ] travel sized products
- [ ] expired bath / body products
- [ ] expired medicine
- [ ] old / used sunscreen
- [ ] toiletries / perfumes
- [ ] use up products
- [ ] under the sink
- [ ] sink area
- [ ] towels

Wardrobe

Spare Buttons

It could be a jar, a drawer or still attached to the clothing, but spare buttons come in their hundreds. If you have ever used or are likely to use them then it is valid to keep them, but if you have buttons for clothing items you no longer have, is it worth keeping them? If you have a friend or family member that does crafting, they may take them in or send in a bag to the local school for art supplies.

Hangers

As you start decluttering your wardrobe you will find that you have far more hangers then is humanly possible to use. Reduce these down by keeping your favourites and getting rid of any broken ones, or any excess.

Hangers the Wrong Way

A trick, if you are not sure which items you wear regularly in your wardrobe, is to turn the hangers the wrong way round. As you use an item, you return it with the hanger facing the right way. After a period of time (of your choosing) you can see which items you wear regularly and which items are sitting there unused that could be donated or sold.

Coats

Having a range of coats can be helpful if you experience a range of different weather, but do we need every style and colour? Coats are much better at lasting, so choose your favourites that you love and declutter any that are either damaged or not being used. Coats can take up a large amount of space and can change the look of the hallway if the selection is smaller.

Costume Jewellery

Not everyone is a jewellery fan, but if you are, consider which pieces are versatile and go with a number of outfits. Keep quality over quantity and items that you love. Trying to keep up with the latest trends is going to keep this collection larger than necessary.

Jewellery

A similar category but worthy of its own area as this is often more sentimental. You will, of course, have pieces that you love, but don't feel guilty about selling an item that was a gift, if it is not something you will ever wear. Jewellery can be very personal in choice and style, so make sure you only keep pieces that you enjoy wearing and you will make the most of.

Don't Let Clothes Pile Up

After a long day, it can be easy to throw clothes in a pile on the floor, on a chair or at the end of the bed. If you absolutely can't do it at night, get in the habit of putting them away every morning. Otherwise, you end up with clothes mountains taking over the room which can be overwhelming to look at.

Shoes

I'm sure most women could spend a large amount of time sorting through this area. I'm not so bothered by having new shoes and often spend money on quality pairs of shoes, trainers and boots but have one of each style only. If you are not like me, then consider first sorting the shoes into different categories, such as sandals, trainers, flipflops, heels, wedges, etc. From this, you can start to see which ones are similar in style or design and begin reducing down your collection. Immediately remove any that you know are uncomfortable or don't fit well, as these can do more damage to your feet than you would care to know. Keep any that are versatile or neutral in colour as these will likely match with a larger number of outfits.

Socks

Any holey socks have done their time, particularly if you are unable to repair them. It can be easy for them to wear down quickly, so it is worth going through this category a couple of times a year. Make sure you only have styles or sizes that you will regularly use and remove any that you no longer wear.

Underwear

You may have favourites here and it's also worth noting which ones you don't wear. Either because they don't fit or are uncomfortable. These are easy ones to dispose of and cheap enough to replace if you ever need a different size.

Pairs of Gloves

Do you have a collection of gloves ready for winter? If so, could you reduce these down by getting rid of any similar styles or colours. Keep quality gloves and remove any that are damaged or are uncomfortable to wear.

Hats and Scarves

I used to have a basket full of scarves and I'm sure at one point I used to wear them. But I could honestly say that basket had been sat there for years, untouched and unloved. Consider neutral and plain scarves as these will mix and match well with numerous items. Hats are a new thing for me. I love a holiday hat, but finding one that fits my head has always been a challenge. This means that when I find one, it ends up being a keeper. I have one summer and one winter brimmed hat and 2 knitted beanie hats. That seems to work well for me and gives me enough options. Consider reducing down any that don't fit or no longer suit your style.

Swimwear

Swimwear has to be comfortable. That's always my starting point, if they ever become tight or too big then they have to go. When choosing them, I again go for plain or simple patterns so that they don't become unfashionable. Think about your favourites and dispose of any you no longer love.

PJs

With new traditions of buying PJs for Christmas, it can be easy to accumulate more pyjamas than you need. Yes, it can be an item worn a lot (it is for me, that's for sure) but do you need a whole drawer full? I tend to stick with having two pairs — one lighter one for summer and a thicker one for winter. Work out which ones you love and wear often and donate the rest.

Tops

It is worth going through tops on a regular basis. Think about how you use them to mix and match outfits and see if there are any that no longer suit you or you don't like wearing. Do you have any duplicates or similar items that can be reduced down to keep only one of that style or colour? Keep any that are versatile and work with several outfits.

Jumpers/Sweatshirts

This is an area that I can be rather fussy in. They have to fit nicely and not be scratchy. As soon as I get to that point and it's not soft and cozy, they have to go. I try and make sure jumpers are plain in colour so that they work well with different skirts, trousers and dresses alike. Think about which are your favourites and ones that you reach for on a regular basis. Reduce down to essentials only.

Trousers

I find trousers difficult to buy and therefore difficult to let go of. Especially if I am in love with the style or colour. But sometimes it is better to be honest with yourself and admit defeat when they no longer fit or suit your style. If the colour is starting to fade or there is damage, consider whether it is worth keeping.

Glasses/Sunglasses

It can be easy to rack up a collection of sunglasses, particularly if you have them stored in different places, such as the car. I tend to only keep ones that are super comfy and that have a dark enough tint to them. Anything else, for me, has to go. Think about which ones are your favourites and reduce down your collection and make sure they are stored safely in cases, if possible. For glasses, I tend to only buy new prescription ones once every two years; if necessary. If that happens then I will dispose of the old ones so that I only have one spare pair.

Workwear

For workwear, it may be that you have a specific uniform or you create a work capsule wardrobe for yourself. Either way, it is important to make sure that it fits well and that it is relevant to your current employment. If you have workwear items from a previous job, then it's time to return these to your old employer.

Dresses

Dresses are a staple in my wardrobe, but I do try and make sure that they are comfy and used regularly. If I find that they are not being used within 6 months or a year it is worth considering donating or selling to raise some additional funds. Decide whether they still suit your style and fit your current body shape and size.

Belts and Ties

I used to buy novelty ties for my dad every Christmas as a child. What was I thinking? He used to wear them, but hopefully he has now let go of these. Unless you are regularly wearing ties, consider keeping a core selection and disposing of the remainder. If you are thinking about sentimental items from loved ones, my mum made a fabulous cushion using old ties, that belonged to my grandad, which became a lovely keepsake. With regards to belts, make sure they fit and are in good condition and consider decluttering any that do not fit or are worn down.

Watches

There are differing views on watches. Some like to have a collection of different styles and colours to work with different outfits, whilst others keep just a few. Whatever your preference, make sure you only keep what you use and sell any that you no longer wear or don't suit your style.

Fancy Dress

I've done a few fancy dress parties, but my stance is that I will probably only wear it once. I usually try and sell my outfit after wearing it or try and borrow in the first place. You can hire costumes these days, so it could be a sustainable option moving forward.

Slippers

If you are a slipper fan (and my son is) then you probably wear them to the bitter end. Make sure you throw out any that are falling apart at the seams and if you get new ones as gifts, only keep ones that you find comfortable and will definitely wear.

WARDROBE
CHECKLIST

- [ ] spare buttons
- [ ] hangers
- [ ] hangers the wrong way
- [ ] coats
- [ ] costume jewellery
- [ ] jewellery
- [ ] don't let clothes pile up
- [ ] shoes
- [ ] socks
- [ ] underwear
- [ ] pairs of gloves
- [ ] hats and scarves
- [ ] swimwear
- [ ] pjs
- [ ] tops

- [ ] jumpers / sweatshirts
- [ ] trousers
- [ ] glasses / sunglasses
- [ ] workwear
- [ ] dresses
- [ ] belts and ties
- [ ] watches
- [ ] fancy dress
- [ ] slippers

Bedroom

Curtains

Do you have any spare curtains being stored in the linen cupboard or a box under the bed? It's time to dust them off and decide whether they are worth keeping hold of. Some people like to change them up on a regular basis and others just like to have a spare that fit just in case. Either way, consider whether you definitely need to keep them and whether you are likely to use them again.

Bedside Table

This is a hot spot for clutter at times. It can easily pile up with drinks glasses or jewellery. It may be that this is an area that is routinely cleared away each day, either in the morning or night. Ensure that things are put away in the drawer and that the drawer is not turning into a junk drawer of randomness. If you have a small library piling up on the top, consider which ones you are going to read first and put the others back on the original bookshelf that they came from.

Bedsheets

I like to have one on and one in the wash. I don't tend to have seasonal or Christmas sets. This might be worth thinking about, for the future, whether you really need different patterns for different seasons, etc. Seasonal ones are likely to be used only a handful of times a year and the rest of the time they end up being sat in storage. Consider keeping ones that suit any season and that match your décor appropriately.

Under the Bed

This can end up being what you think is a trove of treasures, often nostalgic items or seasonal items, depending on your storage set up. Decide what items you will keep in this area and find new homes for the other things. For sentimental items, it may be worth allocating extra time for this. I had a collection of old toys, CDs and photos under the bed and so it took me a little while to appreciate the things I had and decide which to let go of, but it was worth it. I now only have a few sentimental items kept there and that's about it.

Bedroom Floor

It can be easy for the bedroom floor to become a dumping ground of clothes and bits and pieces. It is worth creating new habits of putting clothes away each night to avoid them piling up. It can also be a sign that there are too many items in your wardrobe if it feels like a chore putting it away.

Dressing Table

A dressing table is a must for most bedrooms (unless you are fortunate enough to have a separate room for this). It can be an easy option for leaving things out or for shoving things into drawers and in the space underneath. Aim to keep the surface clear on top and ensure that everything is contained within the drawers in an organised fashion, perhaps using small trays to separate different items. If you need to store things underneath, consider using baskets as a way to contain and store essential items. Remove anything that is not being utilised on a regular basis.

BEDROOM
CHECKLIST

- [ ] curtains
- [ ] bedside table
- [ ] bedsheets
- [ ] under the bed
- [ ] bedroom floor
- [ ] dressing table

Living Area

Vases

Do you have any awkward vases that don't fit the flowers you buy or any styles that don't suit your home. These are great items to donate or sell on. Only keep ones that you love and will use often.

Candles and Wax Melts

I am definitely guilty of having a lot of candles, but I have gotten better over time. I actually no longer buy candles and will not start a new one until I have burnt through the one I am using to the bitter end. Which is absolutely how it should be. I love candles and burn them often, but I am also willing to let them go if I don't like the scent. I will regift any that are not to my liking. With wax melts, it can be easy to accumulate a lot of paraphernalia, but make sure you only keep what you love and is essential.

Cushions and Throws

Changing cushions and throws is certainly cheaper than buying a new sofa! But what happens to the old ones? They end up in storage somewhere in your home. Perhaps seasonal cushions or Christmas throws. Most of the time they are forgotten about and left for years untouched. If you haven't used them, accept that you probably won't in the future and pass them on to someone who will enjoy them and make the most of them. When buying in the future, look for neutrals or ones that will go with a range of colour schemes in your home.

Ornaments

If you love collecting ornaments, then this may be a challenging area. This is also an easy way to see a change in the visual clutter of your home. Reducing down collections or displaying them in a more contained way (such as a display cabinet) can help to manage the collection that you have.

Stairs/Under The Stairs

This is an area that should mostly be clear of clutter, particularly on the stairs. It can too easily become a hazard when we start storing things on the stairs, rather than just putting them where they need to go. Under the stairs can be a trap for a range of miscellaneous items, but make sure you go through this regularly and dispose of anything that is not being used.

Hallway

Many UK households have rather small hallways, so this area can be vital to keep clear. If you have any storage cupboards or console tables, ensure they only have necessary items on them and that they are not overfull. The hallway should be clear of visual clutter.

Dining Table

The ultimate clutter trap is the dining table. It starts with a few unopened letters, followed by a pile of laundry, then toys that have been picked up from the floor. Before you know it, your dining table is lost to clutter and no longer useable for family meals. Make this a priority hotspot for clearing away. Consider which items keep creeping onto it and work out whether there is a reason, or a solution to this.

Pet Toys

Pet toys can easily clutter up the floor and often end up being unused. Consider rotating pet toys so that some are out and some are contained in a drawer. This will be more interesting for the pet and likely to see them being used more. Dispose of any that are broken or absolutely not played with.

Bookshelf

A tough one, but a good way to reduce visual clutter. Declutter any books that you have already read or do not intend to read any time soon. These could be donated to your local library or 'little library' if you have one close to you. You can always borrow these again when you do want to read them. Also think about any ornaments or items stored around the books and whether they really need to be there.

Coffee Table

I'm not a big fan of coffee tables (I prefer a foot stool) but if you do have one, think about what items are essential and should be kept on display and which items you want stored out of sight. Any items that are kept on display, could you contain these in an area so that it is more visually appealing?

Home Décor Items

Decorative items can really make a place feel like home. Always keep items you absolutely love, but decide whether there are any that you could donate or sell. Having too many can easily clutter up the home.

DVDs

I don't keep many DVDs these days. I have just a few of my absolutely favourite films that I watch over and over. It can be good to keep these if you are not subscribing to any film services. But also think about whether they would get watched or sit unopened.

Framed Pictures

I love framed pictures, but only if they are contained to an area. Modern, small houses no longer come with mantels, so it ends up being shelves or units that hold these. I think it's great to display photos, but I love to keep updating with new photos over the years. Whatever your preference, decide whether you are happy with the amount on display and whether they are visually appealing to you.

CDs

CDs are becoming less fashionable by the hour, but I love the freedom of having a CD in the car (I should probably modernise!). I have only a handful of CDs now, a few sentimental ones from my teenage years, but the reality is they are easy to listen to online, either for free or at a small cost. Decluttering CDs can free up a large amount of space in your home.

If you have artwork on display, then it's important to review what you have and how it makes you feel on a regular basis. It's good to switch things up or move things around as and when. Ensure that any art on display works well in the space, as well as being meaningful to you or family members.

LIVING AREA
CHECKLIST

- ☐ vases
- ☐ candles and wax melts
- ☐ cushions and throws
- ☐ ornaments
- ☐ stairs / under the stairs
- ☐ hallway
- ☐ dining table
- ☐ pet toys
- ☐ bookshelf
- ☐ coffee table
- ☐ home decor items
- ☐ DVDs
- ☐ framed pictures
- ☐ CDs
- ☐ art

Children

Toys

Toys may feel like an all-consuming category. I can assure you that children need much less than you think. In fact, the less the better. This is because from having little, comes creativity. Something that is essentially free. Regularly go through and remove any as they break or get damaged. Bundle up toys that are not played with very often and consider donating or selling. When buying toys in future, consider the versatility of the item and whether it will add value to the child's life, rather than allow every little bit of plastic you think they might like. It's about being conscious.

Clothes

Clothing should be checked through twice a year. I tend to do this in the new year and just at the end of summer. Bundle up ages together to make it easy to sell or donate. They grow so quickly that twice a year is probably about right. Bundles of clothing will be easier to sell than individual items.

Consoles

If you have games consoles for your children, ensure that they don't keep anything that they don't play with. Trading old, unused consoles or games is a great way to teach them about how to reuse and recycle and the funds can be used to purchase a new game etc.

Furniture

Think about how much furniture is being utilised to its full potential within your children's bedroom. Make sure items are practical and being used. Reduce down what is being stored in them and use as little furniture as possible so that there is more space to play.

Children's Keepsakes

If you're wondering about the sentimental items, a memory or keepsake box is the way to go. However, the rule is that each child has one box and you must choose the most important things to keep. If you're finding it hard to select items, think about the meaning behind why you are keeping it and choose a range of items that can help to tell a story to your child when they are older.

Children's Books

Children's books were easily accumulated in my household, especially when I started teaching. A wealth of books on the shelf is fantastic for children's growth and development, but so is the library. Buying books is important but as your children grow, so will their tastes. Keep sifting through and taking out any that are no longer age appropriate. You could donate these to friends or family members, as well as your local school or children's centre.

CHILDREN CHECKLIST

- ☐ toys
- ☐ clothes
- ☐ consoles
- ☐ furniture
- ☐ children's keepsakes
- ☐ children's books

Office

Ink Cartridges

Any old or used ink cartridges can be recycled at local supermarkets or through various recycling schemes. Just search online to see what your local area offers. Make sure you don't have any cartridges for old printers.

Notebooks

I love a good notebook, don't you? The difficulty I have is using them, specifically, marking the first page. I end up having so many that they never get used. I get lured in with fancy covers and gilded pages. Be honest with yourself and reduce down to keep just one or two, the rest can be sold or recycled. There's only so many notebooks one person can have.

Magazines

Many people collect magazines for a variety of different interests. If you are keeping them, think about why that is. Is it for a particularly article and could this be cut out of the magazine and the remainder recycled? Consider whether it is ok for you to recycle after reading and why it is that you hold on to them and often never reread them.

Newspapers

I think there are different camps when it comes to newspapers. Some like to keep them to document events or occasions, whilst others tend to recycle them, eventually when they get close enough to the bin. Again, decide whether it is possible to keep the article rather than the whole paper and create a system that works for recycling them more efficiently rather than storing them in piles for a few weeks first.

Junk Mail

An easy way to declutter junk mail is to deal with it straight away, as soon as it lands on the doorstep. Decide whether it is something that is of interest, if not pop it straight into the recycling bin.

Old Calendars

It can be easy to keep hold of calendars longer than necessary, especially when transitioning each year to a new one. The key to not holding on, is to make sure you transfer any important info and dates over straight away. Designate some time to do this and then you are ready to recycle the old one.

Receipts

Depending on whether we are talking business or personal receipts, you may need to keep hold of them for longer than you'd like. It is worth having a simple system in place to contain these, such as a folder or plastic wallet for each month of the year. Make sure you only keep relevant ones. For personal finances, track receipts in a budget planner, but dispose of them immediately afterwards. Don't let them pile up.

Pens and Pencils

I'm a stationary addict! I had a drawer full of all sorts of pens, pencils and stationary equipment. The truth is, it never got used. Well most of it didn't. Remove any that you are unlikely to use, these could be donated to a business or school. Be realistic about what you keep and avoid buying any more until you start using up what you have!

Unused Devices

If you have any tablets, PCs or laptops that are not being used, then think about whether you really need to keep them. These are a great item to sell for some extra funds, or you could donate to a school or charity.

Office Desk/Drawers

Organised chaos is fine, until it becomes unorganised chaos. Recognising the difference can be tough, but a regular clear out of the drawers and top of the desk is worth the effort. It can help you find a sense of calm and you will begin to discover what systems can be put in place to make the space more efficient in the long term.

Old Diaries

I think there are mixed feelings about letting go of old diaries. To clarify, diaries are just dated books with to do lists and events mapped out. Journals, I have added this to the sentimental category as I see these slightly differently. Unless you have a reason to keep them, it is worth letting go each time you get a new one. Like calendars, they have served their purpose and soon become redundant.

Utility Bills

I have very few paper utility bills come through the post now, which I love. It is easy to set up online billing and these can be downloaded each month and stored on a PC or laptop. This takes away some of the faff that comes with paper bills and having to physically process and store them. You can also easily access old bills either through the online services or by asking for paper copies to be sent if you are requiring them for evidence, etc.

Invitations

I love seeing invitations displayed and enjoy the subsequent anticipation of the event, but often, those invitations remain on display for many months after the event. Check through them and dispose of any that have passed already.

Gift Bags

I accumulate a lot of gift bags throughout the year, which can be nice. But it also takes up a lot of space. I tend to keep just a couple of plain or universal gift bags and dispose of the rest. I don't often use them myself and try and reuse ones as much as possible.

Manuals

I used to love reading manuals before using the product. I'm not sure everyone feels the same as me, but they have definitely served a purpose. My go to is to throw them in one box, along with electrical cables, to be stored forever. The reality is, after the first look through, when I am learning about the product, I don't often go back to it. Most manuals for devices can now be found online by searching the manufacturer and product. Digital copies can be accessed and downloaded, if necessary.

Old Phone Books

Gone are the days of receiving a phone book with a list of local and national businesses in. Search engines and the internet have made everything accessible at the click of a button, which is fantastic. This means if you have any old phone books lying around, get them recycled.

Outdated Reference Books

If you have done any studying over the years, you may find that some of the information or data has become outdated and new theories have revolutionised your field. Make sure that reference books are recent and dispose of any that are outdated or unlikely to be used by you in the coming years.

Travel Books/Guides

Travel books are almost becoming obsolete. I have recently started travelling more and so much is available on apps, that the books become an inconvenience to carry. So much has been and gone over the last 5 to 10 years, that many might not have up to date information. Check on search engines and online travel sites for the most up to date information.

Old School Books

I don't know about you, but I had lots of my old school books stored in my parents attic and was quite overwhelmed when they were handed over. It was hard to know what to do with them, so they got left in a box. I recently looked through them and realized that the content wasn't of much help in being able to understand the subject, so ended up being useless. I thought they might help with supporting my son during high school, but really things have changed a lot since then. Be realistic about whether you really need to keep these. The same can be said for your own children's school books when they come home each year. I tend to have a flick through and then recycle them.

OFFICE CHECKLIST

- ☐ ink cartridges
- ☐ notebooks
- ☐ magazines
- ☐ newspapers
- ☐ junk mail
- ☐ old calendars
- ☐ receipts
- ☐ pens and pencils
- ☐ unused devices
- ☐ office desk / drawers
- ☐ old diaries
- ☐ utility bills
- ☐ invitations
- ☐ gift bags
- ☐ manuals
- ☐ old phone books
- ☐ outdated reference books
- ☐ travel books/guides
- ☐ old school books

Bags

Purse/Old Cards

I regularly have a check through of my purse. Once a month is a great starting point. Remove any expired cards or loyalty cards that you are unlikely to use. You may find some old receipts that need filing. Doing this once a month will help you keep on top of it.

Hand Bags

There are two elements to this section. Firstly, do you have too many? Yes, I know many people collect these, but could you find a way to reduce down and keep favourites that you use all of the time? Secondly, regularly clear out your bag to make sure there isn't any clutter in there building up. It will help you to reset and put things back in the right place.

Keyrings/Keys

Check your key bundle and make sure you only have essential keys on there. Do you have any additional keyrings that can be removed so that there is less to carry?

Back Packs/School bags

How many backpacks do you have and do you need to declutter any old or worn ones that you no longer use? Regularly check through your bags for clutter and remove anything that is not needed.

Beach Bags

I love a good beach bag and have been known to buy a new one on each holiday. However, if you find a good one, it is worth making the effort to use it at every opportunity rather than having multiple.

Travel Luggage

Travel bags are essential, but do you have the right sized bags for cabin and hold that work well to the weight restrictions. Think about keeping the right number you will need and get rid of any old ones that you no longer use.

BAGS
CHECKLIST

- [ ] purse / old cards
- [ ] hand bags
- [ ] keyrings / keys
- [ ] back packs / school bags
- [ ] beach bags
- [ ] travel luggage

Beauty

Old Nail Polish

It doesn't take long for old nail polish to start separating. However, if it doesn't mix again when you shake it around, then it's not worth keeping.

Old Products/Expired

Make up has a shelf life. Each item shows a little number on the packaging of how long they should be used for once opened. Use this as a guide. This is most important for any product that go near your eyes, such as mascara and eye shadows. Every 6 months is the norm for eye products to keep healthy and it's not worth taking any risks.

Unused Items

Beauty boxes and advertisements can make it easy for us to stock pile on a number of items that we don't ever use. Numerous palettes and creams can be overwhelming to look at. Consider donating any unopened products that you are unlikely to use.

Hair Accessories

I always reach for the same 2 or 3 hair clips and yet I used to own a whole basket full of them. It's surprising how many accessories we collect each year, and it's important to recognise what is worth purchasing moving forward.

Hair Styling Tools

The current craze is heatless curlers. Let's be honest, how many have you tried? And are they still sitting in the same cupboard unused because they didn't quite work or were uncomfortable to use? Or do you have several hair straighteners or curling tongs? Consider keeping your favourites that you know you will use on a regular basis.

BEAUTY CHECKLIST

- ☐ old nail polish
- ☐ old products / expired
- ☐ unused items
- ☐ hair accessories
- ☐ hair styling tools

Garden and Shed

Bikes and Scooters

As children grow, it is easy to get caught up in buying newer bikes and scooters for them to enjoy and learn to ride. Make sure you consider selling or donating the old one first before a new one enters the garden/shed space. For adult bikes, do you have more than necessary and do you use them?

Garden Tools

There aren't many gardening tools in my shed, just the basics. So why not keep it to that. Consider which tools you have used over the last year. If you haven't even looked at it or used it, then now is the time to sell these.

DIY Supplies

Paint brushes and other DIY supplies should be stored out of reach of children. Consider whether there are any supplies that you are unlikely to use again or anything that is broken or damaged.

Outside Furniture

An easy way to change the cluttered feel of a garden is by removing any unused outside furniture. If you have anything broken or damaged from the weather, then look at the best way to either upcycle or recycle it.

Paint

I am not a fan of keeping old paint. I think its toxic enough, for storing, but also highly flammable. If you know that it is safely stored and sealed (preferably unopened) then you can consider keeping it. But if you know it has been opened for a long time and is not mixable or dried out, then it is time to dispose of it safely at your local recycling centre.

Plant Pots

Somehow I am still finding unused plant pots in the garden and shed (probably due to the plants slowly dying over time). But as I remove the decaying plant remnants, unless I fill it will something new, it becomes unsightly. Many neighbours, friends or family may be in need of some plant pots so empty them out and share them around for others to use.

Plants

If you're anything like me, it might be worth checking your plants are okay. It's time to take out anything that is dying or already a brown twig to make way for some new colourful foliage. Unfortunately, I am also not the best keeper of house plants – so check up on these too.

GARDEN AND SHED CHECKLIST

- ☐ bikes and scooters
- ☐ garden tools
- ☐ DIY supplies
- ☐ outside furniture
- ☐ paint
- ☐ plant pots
- ☐ plants

Car

Car Supplies/Car Care

I often surprised myself with how much car washing stuff I used to have. My car is the one thing I like cleaning. But the reality is, most of it was in the way and not actually being used when I was checking the car and washing it. Consider whether it is worth the space in your home.

Car Boot

Did you know that any extra weight in your car is going to use up more fuel? This is a great reason to get clearing out anything that is unnecessarily being stored in there. Keep it simple and keep only every essentials that you will use in there. For me, that's wellies, first aid kit and reusable shopping bags. Anything else is costing you more than you think to store it there!

Inside of Car

Depending on how you use your car, work or pleasure, can mean that it can easily become a dumping ground for rubbish and miscellaneous items. It can often be helpful to a way to store items that are needed on a storage hanger on the back of the seats for toys or work items. Having a weekly clear out of rubbish can also help to keep on top of this!

Glove Box

It can be easy to accumulate items such as CDs/MP3 players, cables, sunglasses and satellite navigation systems. The glove box should have some key items within it: MOT certificate, notebook and pen (for taking insurance details in case of an accident). Anything else is extra. Keep things organised by reducing down the other items and only storing them there if needs must.

CAR
CHECKLIST

- ☐ car supplies / car care
- ☐ car boot
- ☐ inside of car
- ☐ glove box

Sentimental

Old Birthday and Christmas Cards

I used to keep cards from every birthday and Christmas and I don't think I was alone in this. However, can you honestly say that you ever looked at them or why you kept them? When I looked through each card, it made me realise how generic they can be. Dear so and so, happy birthday, love so and so. They didn't mean anything to me. There were some that had a beautiful message, and those were the few that I kept. They are kept purely for me and my memory and they are items that I would happily have sent to the bin after I pass. They are personal. It is worth having an honest look through and keeping you favourites and disposing of the rest.

Journals

I told you I would come back to journals. This one is going to be entirely up to you. They may document your journey through life that you absolutely want to treasure. My journaling was sporadic at best. My teenage years were a depressing read and for me not something I wanted to relive. Decide if they are worth keeping for you.

Photos

I love a photo album and putting photos into frames and displaying them in my home. It makes me smile. The best advice here is to regularly go through and get rid of duplicates, blurry shots and ones that don't have interesting subject matter in the shot. Organise the rest in a way that works for you, I like to store chronologically or grouped into occasions.

Letters

I had some lovely childhood letters stored away in my parents attic. They were a lovely memory of pen pal writing in my teenage years and much more spritely than the journals. I decided to keep one from each friend and dispose of the rest. The truth is I will never want to read them.

'Just in case' Items

This could be another chapter in itself. Here I am referring to any item that is being kept because you think you might need it at some point. Ask yourself 'how long have I already kept this item?' and 'am I likely to use it in the next few months?'. If you have already been hoarding this away for a long time, accept that it may not be needed. Also dispose of any item that is really easy to get hold of again. These items are replaceable at any time.

Memorabilia

If you like collecting things, particularly memorabilia, then you may have a large number of items. Part of the theory behind collecting is to have one of everything, to be a collector of all. This is fine if you have the space to accommodate this, however if you are not so fortunate, you could consider reducing down your memorabilia to you absolute favourite pieces. You could sell the other items to another collector.

SENTIMENTAL CHECKLIST

- [ ] old birthday and Christmas cards
- [ ] journals
- [ ] photos
- [ ] letters
- [ ] 'just in case' items
- [ ] memorabilia

Challenges

Little Acts of Decluttering

This is it! This little acts of decluttering book is precisely the challenge you have chosen to embark on. A small area to focus in on each day to help you make progress over time in a manageable, achievable way. For more support with this, I share a calendar PDF (on my website, www.declutteryourlife.co.uk) with suggested little acts of decluttering for each day of the month, for a randomised approach. Otherwise, you could choose a room at a time to focus on or pick randomly yourself.

Fill a Box

Each day you fill a box with items that could be removed from your home. You could put items that are broken, rubbish, or things you no longer use or need. But each day you have to remove it too. Don't let the box sit there too long before you donate it.

10 minutes-10 spaces-100 items

The maths has been done for you here. 100 items in ten days. Just set a 10 minute timer and see how quickly you can find 10 items. Game on! This game could be played with family members at the same time. First to find their 10 items wins.

5 Min Declutter Daily

Setting a daily timer is a fun way to chip away at an area without the pressure of knowing that it needs to be completed. Taking on a whole room can be daunting, so clearing what you can in 5 minutes becomes less of a daunting task and something that is achievable. This might cover clearing through a junk drawer or cutlery drawer.

15 Min Timer

If you want to get a bit more achieved you could up the timer from 5 minutes to 15 minutes. This will help you see a quicker impact and would work well on slightly bigger areas, like a bedside cabinet, or a small bookcase. You could get some music playing in the background to tune you in and make it more enjoyable.

Bin Bag

This is a great challenge if you are just starting in your decluttering journey. Grab a bin bag and go through your home or an area and find anything that is just rubbish, such as packets, receipts, broken items and put the bag straight in the main bin outside when you're done.

Find X Items

A great way to get the whole family involved is to get each person to find a certain number of items to declutter (items to be sold, donated or rubbish). First one to reach the number is the winner. This also works well as an individual task. You could challenge yourself to increase the number of items decluttered each time.

12-12-12 Challenge

This is a simple activity: find 12 items to throw away, 12 items to donate and 12 items to be returned to their proper home. This is a challenge that could be done as and when you choose, or daily to help declutter and tidy each time.

30 Day Minimalism Game

This is a great way to tackle a large number of items in a month. 465+ to be exact! For each day of the month you declutter the number of items for that date. On the first of the month, 1 item decluttered; for the second of the month, 2 items; the third day of the month, 3 items and so on. There are some strategies you can apply to make this manageable. For large number of items think small or cluttered areas of the home, such as stationary or the wardrobe. For smaller numbers of items such as 1-5 you may wish to focus on larger items such as furniture or appliances.

30 DAY
Minimalism Game

DAY 1	DAY 2	DAY 3	DAY 4	DAY 5
☐ 1 item	☐ 2 items	☐ 3 items	☐ 4 items	☐ 5 items
DAY 6	**DAY 7**	**DAY 8**	**DAY 9**	**DAY 10**
☐ 6 items	☐ 7 items	☐ 8 items	☐ 9 items	☐ 10 items
DAY 11	**DAY 12**	**DAY 13**	**DAY 14**	**DAY 15**
☐ 11 items	☐ 12 items	☐ 13 items	☐ 14 items	☐ 15 items
DAY 16	**DAY 17**	**DAY 18**	**DAY 19**	**DAY 20**
☐ 16 items	☐ 17 items	☐ 18 items	☐ 19 items	☐ 20 items
DAY 21	**DAY 22**	**DAY 23**	**DAY 24**	**DAY 25**
☐ 21 items	☐ 22 items	☐ 23 items	☐ 24 items	☐ 25 items
DAY 26	**DAY 27**	**DAY 28**	**DAY 29**	**DAY 30**
☐ 26 items	☐ 27 items	☐ 28 items	☐ 29 items	☐ 30 items

General

Storage Boxes

Now that we have reduced down the unnecessary items in your home, it's time to reduce down all of the storage boxes being used. These are great items to sell on for some easy money as they hold their value. Keeping them means you are more likely to fill the boxes with random items that you want to keep. Keep decluttering the storage boxes from your home as you empty them.

Windowsills

Windowsills are often breeding grounds for clutter. They collect knick-knacks, photo frames and for the most part dust. The ability to keep these areas clean and dust free is often hindered due to the sheer task of needing to remove everything, then cleaning and then the challenge of putting it all back in the same place. Reducing down what is displayed here can really make a difference to the overall look and feel of the home. Being able to easily clear and clean the surfaces will make a difference to how you feel in the space, particularly if you think about having the windows open to let air circulate the room.

Attic

The attic can be a treasure chest or a burden of junk. You can make the judgement call on that one. This may be a longer area to work on, but worth the time. If you are thinking about what items you would want family members to have, consider having the conversation with them about this. Never assume that someone will want it. You could be storing something that isn't wanted. Go through a box at a time and consider what is worth keeping for you and what items make you happy.

Coins/Change Jar

I have fond memories of counting 2p's and 1p's at my Grandad's house when I was little. And if that is something that you are using them for, then I wouldn't dream of taking that joy away. Think about their purpose and what you are using them for. We live in a largely cashless society, so do you need to be keeping hold of loose change? Unless it is serving a purpose, consider going to the bank and putting it into an account. That's the best place for your money to be, particularly if you are wanting it for savings.

Batteries

Any old batteries are not going to be safe to use. Make sure they are stored safely to prolong their life. But any that are showing signs of damage should be recycled. Most UK supermarkets have a battery recycling box available for you to put them in.

Light Bulbs

Check through any spare bulbs that you have and check that they fit the current fixtures in your home or car. They are easily broken, so make sure that they are stored carefully and dispose of any that you are unlikely to use.

Small Appliances

We have talked kitchen appliances, but do you have any other small appliances that are surplus to requirements? This is a great way to earn some additional money by selling them on. This is going to free up some valuable space too.

Have a Donation Box

Another strategy for decluttering regularly is to have a box (somewhere central) that can be filled with items that you want to donate as you find them. Then, when the box is full, you can take it along to your local charity shop to donate.

Duplicates

It can be easy to have duplicate items within your home. We forget what we have brought or have a couple of the same items, such as charging cables, to make it easier to charge multiple items at once. Think about the duplicate items and whether you really need more than one. Or can you reduce down so you have a couple less than before?

Full Drawer

If you are not sure where to start when decluttering, work in one small space at a time. If you have a drawer that is overflowing, this is a sign that it needs reducing down. Declutter enough items so that you can comfortably close the drawer again.

Clear a Surface

To start clearing away the clutter, get in the habit of clearing surfaces around your home. There will be many shelves, counter tops, cupboards and tables where clutter might build up. Find a surface and reduce the clutter or clear it completely. Aim to either find everything a home, or dispose of what you no longer need.

Touch Things Only Once

Reducing visual clutter can be tough. But if you think about every time you move something, but not finish what you should do, it just becomes a postponed job or decision that needs addressing. Touching items only once is a good habit that encourages you to make sure you put things properly away when you are finished with the item. Wash the dishes or load the dishwasher as soon as you finish serving up. Put the opened envelopes straight into the recycling bin, rather than on the side or by the door. By doing those small jobs straight away, you will reduce the amount of visual clutter that builds up in daily life.

90/90 Rule

The 90/90 rule means you need to ask yourself have you used the item in the last 90 days and/or do you intend to use it in the next 90 days? If you answer yes, then it's a keeper. If not, then it is time to say goodbye.

Would You Buy It Again?

This is a great question to ask yourself when decluttering items. If the answer is yes, then it is worth keeping that item or that kind of item. If the answer is no, consider either decluttering when it breaks or declutter it now if it makes you think that you might not use it again.

Limit Space

If you are finding that you have too many of a certain item, try putting limitations on the amount of space occupied by it. For example, you could say that you are only allowed one drawer for t-shirts. Your aim would then be to declutter enough t-shirts so that the ones you keep will all fit in that drawer. Limiting the space you have for a category can help to encourage tougher decision making.

Home For Everything

Some people think I am asking a big thing here, but I tend to disagree. I don't expect everything to be immediately found the correct place to live, but as you work through each area and begin putting items back, it is worth noting how and where you use the item and make sure it's place works for how you use it.

Ask – Does It Make You Happy?

This is the key to decluttering. The aim is to fill your home with all of the things that make you happy. This is a great question to ask about each item when decluttering, so that you are reassured about the fact that the goal is to keep what you love and remove what you don't.

1 in 1 Out Policy

This is a great way to keep a limit on the number of items in your home whilst you are still decluttering, as well as a great strategy moving forward. If you buy a new top, you must choose an old one to donate or recycle. This works well for children's artwork. A new picture on the fridge means an old one must be removed. It prevents additional clutter or additional items from being added to your home.

Spare Cables

You could be in one of two camps here. The cable drawer/box camp (that's me!) or the cables everywhere (help me find the right one). But both options are guilty of having multiple cables unnecessarily, as well as cables to fit... well I'm not quite sure what they connect with. 'Is that even a connector that's used these days?' Reducing down the number of duplicate cables is the first step and then any that don't match up to a device. Cables are so easy to purchase these days that this can be easily replaced if broken or damaged, but keeping a stock of 10 is perhaps a step too far?

Junk Drawer

We all love a junk drawer. Whether it be for an easy 'throw things in' or a way to hide the mess. Depending on your usage these can be a blessing or a curse. Sometimes it's best to have a partially organised junk drawer. Think about the items that usually find their way here and consider if there is somewhere more suitable they could live in the house. Go through and remove any rubbish hiding in there or items that are of now use. Anything that is left could these be organised into categories and separated into smaller containers? Do you need a junk drawer at all and so could you utilize the space in a different way?

Furniture

We often have more furniture than we need in a space. The living room can feel cluttered with different side tables and coffee tables. The bedroom can have wardrobes and several chest of drawers and bedside tables. All of these can make the space look small and unusable. Reducing down some of the furniture (which will mean reducing what is stored in there too), will help to open up the space, as well as reduce the opportunity for clutter to build up on the surfaces.

Gift Cards/Coupons

Gift cards are a great gift, especially to a minimalist who is particular about what enters their home. However, don't let the cards sit in your purse for an eternity. Decide what your plan is for the gift card and get this actioned. It would be a shame if any were wasted. Coupons are a fab way to save money on a range of items. However, it is important not to get caught up in the excitement of random products that you won't necessarily use. Use up coupons and give away any that you are unlikely to use. Someone else may benefit from this.

GENERAL CHECKLIST

- [ ] storage boxes
- [ ] windowsills
- [ ] attic
- [ ] coins / change jar
- [ ] batteries
- [ ] light bulbs
- [ ] small appliances
- [ ] have a donation box
- [ ] duplicates
- [ ] full drawer
- [ ] clear a surface
- [ ] touch things only once
- [ ] 90 / 90 rule
- [ ] would you buy it again?
- [ ] limit space
- [ ] home for everything
- [ ] ask - does it make you happy?
- [ ] 1 in 1 out policy
- [ ] spare cables
- [ ] junk drawer
- [ ] furniture
- [ ] gift cards / coupons

Phone

Contact List/Friends

It always surprises me when I see people with a thousand friends on social media or in their contacts list. Not because I'm jealous, but more down to not being able to see the wood for the trees. I keep the bestest, most important people in my life and I love to see what they are up to and keep in touch with them. That would be difficult to do if my page was flooded with a thousand different people that I met once or would never speak to if I passed them in the street. Reducing down my contacts list and friends to my core group helped me to focus on those relationships with more purpose, direction and happiness.

Apps

Often, we can clutter our phones up with an array of different apps for a variety of reasons and for the most part, they are taking up valuable storage space. Consider which apps you are using and whether it is worth keeping the rest. This will reduce down the number of notifications (see next section), but also the visual aesthetics of your phone. If you want to improve this further, create folders for your apps to live within. I have affirmations as headers for mine; I am connected, I am healthy, etc. and the relevant apps go under each affirmation.

Notifications

As a standard, notifications are automatically turned on when we download a new app. But when you start to have a larger number of apps notifying you of random things, it can become overwhelming. The noise can often cause stress and anxiety if it is overused and creates this added layer of noise that is unnecessary, for the most part. I agree that some notifications are important, like text and calls, but do we really need to have our phone alert us for every little thing on social media? Take control by only getting the notifications when already in the app. This makes it feel more manageable and gives you back control.

Duplicate Photos

The growth of digital cameras means that we are constantly snapping our favourite people and things. With that, we can get trigger happy and have far too many photos of the same set up. Consider deleting or decluttering any duplicates, blurry shots or ones that just don't look that interesting anymore.

Old Phones

Do you have any old phones lying around? This is a good item to try and sell and make some additional money from. Avoid upgrading to the latest phone each year and see if you can last a few more years before changing it up.

PHONE
CHECKLIST

- [ ] contact list / friends
- [ ] apps
- [ ] notifications
- [ ] duplicate photos
- [ ] old phones

Seasonal

Christmas Decorations

I love a Christmas bauble and if I see a nice one at the Christmas market, it will be the only thing purchased. I like to keep the same colour scheme so that each year I reuse the same decorations. I can move things around for variety, but it is mostly the same. Here it depends on your preferences. If you love decorating then consider what is visually appealing to you and go through your collection each year and remove anything you haven't used or are unlikely to use so that you are keeping on top of this.

Halloween Decorations

Keep it simple. I'm not a fan of this holiday personally, but I know the kids love it. It is possible to celebrate and join in with the fun without purchasing too much, so keep the decorations simple and ones that are useable each year.

Easter Decorations

Easter trail decorations and spring time paraphernalia can easily add up, especially if you have young kids. Avoid adding to your collection each year and keep only the essentials if you are adamant about keeping them. Having a teenager means that the magic of Easter is gone for us, so these have all been donated.

Unused Gifts

The guilt of letting go of a gift is tough. We want to keep it because of the memory attached and we get hung up on thinking that losing the gift means losing the memory. When it's a gift you don't like or don't use, it is ok to let this go. And if anyone asks why you let it go you can just say that it wasn't to your liking.

Travel Items/Bags

Travel specific items are helpful if you are using them regularly. It can be easy to buy additional items that you don't really use and feel the need to hold on to them 'just in case'. Excess bags are going to be taking up space in your home, so keep your favourites and sell or donate the rest. Travel specific items such as travel sized products should be used up straight after the trip if there is any left over and avoid picking up additional ones from hotels and accommodation. You really don't need it and will be unlikely to use it.

Pool Inflatables

Every time I used to go on holiday, a new pool inflatable would be purchased. I would often bring these all the way home with me in the suitcase, and they would sit in the suitcase for a few years. When getting ready for another holiday, I would then decide not to take them as it takes up too much room in the suitcase. I now have a rule that we pass it on to other guests when we leave our holiday accommodation so that it is not wasted and fully enjoyed.

SEASONAL CHECKLIST

- ☐ Christmas decorations
- ☐ Halloween decorations
- ☐ Easter decorations
- ☐ unused gifts
- ☐ travel items / bags
- ☐ pool inflatables

Hobbies

Board Games/Puzzles

I love a board game, don't you? But how many are just sat there unloved and unplayed. Could it be that some have become outgrown by your children and some may have been played to the ends of time and you're ready for something new. Whatever the reason, it's worth going through this section regularly.

Fitness Equipment

Are there any equipment items that are sat unused? If so, would you consider selling these on? When you know that these items are not being used, think about whether you are willing to continue sacrificing the space in your home being used for these items, that may be best used for something else. Keep what is important and used regularly, and be realistic about the rest.

Half-finished Craft Projects

Hands up if you have a half finished craft project lying around. Hands up if it's more than one! If you're anything like me, I love starting projects. Often, I run out of time, come across an issue or need to purchase something additional to complete it. It then gets put off and put aside, in a box, never to be seen again. It's time to make some harsh decisions here about whether or not you really will finish them any time soon and if not, it's time to say goodbye or find someone who can take this on.

Sports Accessories

If you play a sport, then you will likely have an array of rackets, balls and clothing connected to this sport. If it is a sport that you actively participate in, then consider reducing down any items you don't really use. If you no longer play the sport, or are unlikely to play the sport, then consider donating the equipment to your local school or sports centre for someone else to utilise.

Digital Cameras

If you like photography, then you may have an abundance of accessories or a collection of cameras. Do you have any cameras or items that you no longer use? These items are good for selling to earn some extra cash. Make sure you go through any SD cards or storage bags too.

Craft Accessories

If you love a craft session, then the reality is that you probably have too many craft accessories. Starting a new hobby comes with an array of different bits and pieces being needed. But often we buy more than we need or will ever use. Thinking I might use it on this project or that. This category can often be a larger one than others, so it may be worth going through sections at a time within it and be realistic. Many items could be donated to family or friends or sold on for a bit of money back.

HOBBIES CHECKLIST

- ☐ board games / puzzles
- ☐ fitness equipment
- ☐ half finished craft projects
- ☐ sports accessories
- ☐ digital cameras
- ☐ craft accessories

Additional Resources

Additional information can be found on my social media pages under the name Declutter Your Life.

For more details on decluttering, minimalism and my no spend year, check out my YouTube channel.
https://www.youtube.com/c/RachelNoakes

You can check out my website for blog entries:
www.declutteryourlife.co.uk

I have created a Little Acts of Decluttering Planner available, on Amazon. It contains goal setting pages, declutter checklists and a daily planner to schedule decluttering into your day.

Goal Planner

GOAL

DATE DUE:

ACTION STEPS	BARRIERS

HOW TO OVERCOME BARRIERS

NOTES:

Goal Planner

GOAL

DATE DUE:

ACTION STEPS

BARRIERS

HOW TO OVERCOME BARRIERS

NOTES:

Goal Planner

GOAL

DATE DUE:

ACTION STEPS

BARRIERS

HOW TO OVERCOME BARRIERS

NOTES:

Goal Planner

GOAL

DATE DUE:

ACTION STEPS	BARRIERS

HOW TO OVERCOME BARRIERS

NOTES:

Goal Planner

GOAL

DATE DUE:

ACTION STEPS

BARRIERS

HOW TO OVERCOME BARRIERS

NOTES:

Goal Planner

GOAL

DATE DUE:

ACTION STEPS	BARRIERS

HOW TO OVERCOME BARRIERS

NOTES:

Printed in Great Britain
by Amazon

bc6d0913-948f-47fa-9da9-67b90a1d9e41R01